GOD, HERE'S YOUR STUFF

A Seven Day Devotional to Trusting God
Updated and Expanded

Shirley Hubbard

Copyright © 2015
Shirley Hubbard
All Rights Reserved

ISBN: 0692393714
ISBN-13: 978-0692393710

Unless otherwise indicated, all Scripture quotations are taken from the Holy Bible, New Living Translation copyright © 1996, 2004, 2007, 2013 by Tyndale House Foundation. Used by permission of Tyndale House Publishers, Inc., Carol Stream, Illinois 60188. All rights reserved.

No part of this book may be produced or transmitted in any form or by any means, electronic or mechanical, including photocopying, recording or by any information storage or retrieval system without written permission from the author except for the inclusion of brief quotations in a written review.

LEGAL DISCLAIMER:

Although every precaution has been taken to verify the accuracy of the information contained herein, the author assumes no responsibility for any errors or omissions. No liability is assumed for damages that may result from the use of information contained within.

PERSONAL DISCLAIMER:

Unless a Biblical passage or Biblical reference is included, nothing written here is gospel or carved in stone.

The views expressed here are representative of the author's truth, are sometimes humorous in nature and are intended to help, not offend!

This book was written to help change the way you view your struggle and is

lovingly dedicated to some of the most important people in my life...

My mom, Marie, who consistently and deliberately encourages me to push beyond my self-imposed limitations and never gives up on me even when I want to give up on myself.
You are indeed the wind beneath my wings.

to each of my children:

Jessica, R'Shad, Amber, Asia and Nylah, who unfailingly and affectionately embrace the crazy that is me when I'm in the *writer's cave*. Thank you for saying, "I'm proud of you, mom" when I so desperately needed to hear it! My love for each of you is immeasurable.

to my 'anyway' friend

Dani, who sees what a mess I can be – how moody I am, but wants me in her life anyway! Thanks for always embracing and overlooking the *dysfunction* that is me!!! Here's to changing the way we view our struggle.
LYMI.

and finally to my baby brother

Robert, whom I miss dearly and whose words, "fight for what you want" will forever resonate in my spirit. There is not a day that goes by that I don't long for your presence, but I am so very thankful for the moments we shared while you were here. My love for you will never dissipate. Rest on baby boy.

A special thanks to my *little big brother*, Rod
who always seems to catch me at my weakest moments just in time to
shove me back to the other side of faith

AND

to all of my family and friends for your prayers,
encouragement and support! You color my world beautiful!

Preparation for the Journey

Cleaning the Temple

Mountain Moving - Mustard Seed Faith

Give God His Stuff

Not in Working in Order

It All Works Together

Daily Faith Affirmations

Contents

1	Introduction	
2	Preparation for the Journey What You Need to Know How to Use this Guide Cleaning the Temple	8
3	Mountain Moving, Mustard Seed Faith	14
4	Give God His Stuff	18
5	Day One The Girl in the Mirror	21
6	Day Two As You Sow, You Shall Reap	30
7	Day Three Struggle is Necessary	40
8	Day Four It's Going to Happen Suddenly	50
9	Day Five Just Say the Word	61
10	Day Six Trust the Process	72
11	Day Seven The Answer to Why	81
12	Not in Working Order	91
13	It All Works Together	96
14	Faith Reminders for Life's Challenges	98

When God says He can do exceedingly and abundantly above all we can ask or think, He means it!

Introduction

Allow me to introduce myself – I'm Shirley aka Shirl aka self-proclaimed Microwave Girl. What does that mean? Simply stated, I'm impatient, intolerant and somewhat uncompromising. I want what I want when I want it –quick, fast and in a hurry! That is one of my many flaws and the one that most often leaves me screaming, HURRY UP GOD! I'M WAITING! The problem with that is I usually take matters into my own hands. And the problem with that is, in more cases than not, I end up with a mini – sometimes major catastrophe on my hands. But here's the deal – it's not my fault! I blame society. Here I am in a world of instant gratification, instant food, instant messaging… instant EVERYTHING! How can I not want instant results from a supreme being who is able to do immeasurably more than I can ask or imagine? That's what He says in His word, right? Yep! But, let's get real! Society is most certainly not to blame for my impatience, lack of tolerance or anxiousness. That LITTLE defect is nobody's fault but mine! It has become a huge thorn in my side and is preventing me from walking into my God given destiny.

In my dreams, where everything is as it's supposed to be, I've changed my ways, my patience has grown by leaps and bounds, and I'm more tolerant today than I've ever been in my life. But, in reality, that is furthest from the truth. I'm in the middle of a serious battle with my flesh and the struggle to trust God's process is a very real one. However, what I've learned on my journey to break free of the *I want it now* mindset is that when God says He can do exceedingly and abundantly above all we can ask or think, He means it! We may not always understand why He has us in waiting, but we can rest in the assurance that He always has our best interest at heart and things will start to happen when He knows the time is right. But even that realization isn't always enough for me to trust that God will honor His promises.

As I lay awake on one of my sleepless nights, my thoughts wandered from one place to the next, thinking about all of the extravagant things I want…no…need to happen in my life. As I lay there, listening to the loudness of silence and reflecting on the struggle I was fighting aggressively to win, I began to question if all of these amazingly awesome things could happen in the midst of my current circumstance. In the middle of my questioning…in the middle of my doubting, I heard God's voice, "Do you not believe every word I've spoken is true? Do you not believe there is purpose in your pain? Do you not believe I am who I say I am? Do you not believe my plans are to give you a hope and a future?" I replied, "I do believe, but…" Before I could complete that sentence, He said, "No! You don't believe! You don't believe there is prosperity and greatness on the other side of your struggle. I have laid out a plan tailored made just for you. I've told you exactly what you need to do to bring these things to fruition. You're afraid! You're a procrastinator! You like to make excuses for why these things can't…why these things won't happen to you! You don't have the audacity to take me at my Word!" What could I say? He was right! At that moment, I realized I was suffering from what I like to call *The Doubting Thomas Syndrome.* I knew I was suffering from this horrible illness because the words "I believe" and "but" should never be used in the same sentence when conversing with God. What I was really saying was, *I believe you, but I need physical proof that these things will really happen.*

In my quest to find a cure for my ailment, I journeyed back in time to a few of the events leading up to the crucifixion of Christ. In my mind's eye, I slowly walked up to the crucifix where Jesus was hanging on the cross between two criminals. One of them mocked Him, "You're the Messiah, aren't you? Prove it by saving yourself—and save us too, while you're at it!" But the other criminal objected, "Don't you fear God even when you have been sentenced to die? We deserve to die for our crimes, but this man hasn't done anything wrong." He then uttered some of the most noteworthy words known to mankind, "Jesus, remember me when you come into your Kingdom" (Luke 23: 39-42). This man had the right idea. He was ready to accept the consequences for his behavior and he knew that Jesus hanging next to him was an opportunity for him to be shown favor — thereby gaining eternal life. His counterpart, on the other hand, saw Jesus being there as an opportunity to escape the consequences of his criminal acts and undoubtedly spent his afterlife in the pit of hell.

And then it hit me! An epiphany of epic proportion — my lack of trust or *The Doubting Thomas Syndrome* was directly related to the way I viewed my struggle. That revelation forced me to take a deeper look at why Thomas found it difficult to believe that Jesus had risen from the dead. As I searched for answers, I was taken aback by Thomas' love for Jesus. He loved Him with every fiber of His being and He believed Jesus' love for him was even greater. But what he didn't believe was that a love that great could extend beyond the grave. The resurrection of Christ was incomprehensible to him. Which means he viewed the crucifixion as the end—not the beginning. Likewise, when I'm going *through*, I can't get past my doubt...I can't overcome my fear because I see the circumstance as everything but what it is— an opportunity for growth.

The same, without question, holds true for you. When unpleasant situations arise, instead of saying, *thank You for counting me worthy to fight this battle...Thank You for growing me through this*, you probably find yourself asking every why question imaginable. Don't beat yourself up about it! That reaction is very common among believers, but I'm here to help propel you to your place of victory and the only way to do that is to help you embrace the fact that every experience you encounter is a part of God's divine plan. I know you're probably saying, *that's easier said than done*. That's what the enemy wants you to believe; allow me to correct you on that! Placing limitations on yourself is such a huge waste of time. You can do it just as easily as you say it. You just have to want it badly enough!

Contrary to what the enemy would have you believe, you are NOT powerless!! God has given you authority over every attack of satan, but somewhere down the line, you gave up your power! It's time to put your foot down and take it back! Stop doubting! Doubt is just fear masked in logic! Stop feeding off what appears to be sensible. When has the work of God ever made sense to mankind? Stop operating in disbelief! Stop worrying! Stop walking in fear! No eye has seen... no ear has heard...no mind has imagined what God has prepared for you!!

The battle between the flesh and the spirit can be strenuous. BUT as you grow in the spirit, your flesh looses its power!

Preparation for the Journey

This seven day devotional will take you on a journey of self-awareness and I'll serve as your personal tour guide while sharing some of my personal *I want it now st*ruggles. Here is where you'll learn to rid yourself of that *microwave* mindset in exchange for one of irrefutable trust in God's timing.

Here are a few things you need to get started:

1. A commitment to follow through – if you're serious about escaping the microwave mentality, set aside a specific time for your daily journey and stick to it.

2. Self-honesty – this is the key to self-discovery. If you can't be honest with yourself, your journey will be in vain.

3. A good study Bible – a translation that works best for you.

4. Journal – other than your Bible, your personal journal is THE most important component of this journey. There are daily take-a-ways to help you process the information from each day. Your journal will slowly become your new best friend. Instead of jotting things down on paper or relying on memory, you'll discover how much more effective this transformation can be if you let the journal do the remembering for you. Make a commitment to carrying it with you daily to jot down personal revelations throughout the day. If you prefer not to use a journal, writing space has been provided at the end of each devotional for your thoughts and plan of attack.

What You Need to Know

There are four key elements to escaping the *microwave – I want it now* mindset. Each element is crucial to your journey to patience and endurance. Each one goes hand-in-hand and one simply does not work without the other……..

1. Self-examination is necessary. Examine yourself from the inside out to determine what is hindering your relationship with Christ.

2. Accept responsibility for your role in your current circumstances.

3. Destroy the image in your head of what your life is supposed to look like.

4. Believe God does indeed have plans for your life.

How to Use this Guide

The first four days of this journey will serve as an opportunity for you to thoroughly examine yourself so that you can get to the root of your mistrust issues regarding faith. During the last three days, we'll take a close look at the word "faith" and what it means to you and your Christian walk.

Each devotional is designed to help you change the way you view your struggle. Each day has a scripture to commit to memory, a passage for study and meditation and a guided prayer. Each question is designed to remind you of the amazing miracles God has already worked in your life. These tools will be used in connection with your heart's response to the teachings. Here is where you need to make really good use of your journal. Thoroughly answer each question at the end of the devotional. Don't give a simple yes or no response. Dig deep into the core of your being. Scratch beneath the surface to get a full understanding of God's Word and come up with a plan to apply to your daily life. Take note of the changes that need to be made as a result of the devotional. Make note of other scriptures that can be added to reinforce the scriptures already provided. And last but not least make a commitment to share your findings with others struggling to trust God.

And he said unto them, This kind can come forth by nothing, but by prayer and fasting.

Mark 9:29 KJV

Cleaning the Temple

On my quest to trust God's plans for my life, I often find myself fighting a serious battle with my flesh. With that said, you may want to take this opportunity to do a little *spring cleaning* from the inside out. Although it is not required, you should prayerfully consider a spiritual fast along with this seven-day journey. Biblically speaking, fasting is beneficial and is often associated with abstaining from food, drink or sex. Try not to put too much emphasis on *abstaining from*, but instead on the true purpose of fasting —taking your attention off worldly things to focus completely and wholeheartedly on God. It is the believer's way of demonstrating to God that we are serious about our Christian journey.

This guide was birthed during a seven day hiatus from television and social media taken out of obedience to and under the guidance and direction of God. When it was originally dropped in my spirit, I made every attempt not to plan it around my favorite television shows, but God reminded me that doing so would not be sacrificial. I then made the sacrifice during the season of one my favorite television shows. I'm a *bad television junkie* so doing so was by far one of the most challenging sacrifices I've ever made. But here's how I made it work to my advantage. I used each time frame that was previously allotted for television or social media as a time for prayer, study, and meditation. It was during this time that God revealed the things and people that were hindering my growth and thereby preventing me from reaching my destiny. I used those seven days as the jumpstart to a serious monogamous relationship with God. I didn't spend the entire time telling Him what I wanted or needed Him to do in my life. My relationship with God is just that — a relationship, and in a relationship there is two-way communication. So I learned to listen for guidance and direction, which brought immeasurable joy and in turn made trusting God's process a lot easier! Although fasting is often associated with giving up food, it is essentially about denying the flesh so that God gets the glory in your life. It's about sacrificing or giving up those things that may be hindering your relationship with God. If the Spirit leads you to do so, know that it will take commitment and dedication. It will mean giving up some things you find enjoyable and somewhat difficult to live without. But also know that taking your mind off your fleshly desires, gives you the opportunity to wholeheartedly focus on Christ and His desires for you. It is not to be used as a means of *bribing* God to do what you want. It should be practiced in humility and with a joyful attitude. As difficult as it may seem, everyone can give up something for the benefit of spiritual growth. With fasting comes a new perspective of life's circumstances and a renewed dependence upon God to bring you victoriously to the other side.

Mountain Moving, Mustard Seed Faith

As a babe in Christ at the tender age of fifteen, I didn't really understand mountain-moving or mustard seed faith, but I knew in order for this thing called faith to move mountains with something as tiny as a mustard seed, it had to be pretty powerful. Now that I'm older and wiser and because my faith has been challenged on so many occasions, I fully understand the power of mountain moving, mustard seed faith.

Recently, while basking in the awesomeness of God, I began to think about my nine-year-old granddaughter, who was born prematurely, weighing a little over two pounds. I was immediately taken back to the day I learned my twelve-year-old daughter was pregnant. I was devastated and my flesh wanted to find a way to *get rid* of the child growing inside of her, but my spirit knew I could have no part in terminating the life of an innocent child. My baby was five years old at the time and I had no intentions of going back to the days of staying up all night with a crying infant. The very thought of changing diapers and washing bottles made me nauseous. I just wasn't ready to take care of a baby. So I began to contemplate adoption. But the Lord said, NOT SO!

After much prayer, buckets of tears and countless sleepless nights, I knew without a doubt, the Lord wanted me to raise this baby, but I couldn't see how I would make it happen. I would need a financial miracle to take on an addition to my family. But against my judgment, I began making preparations for this life changing event. I educated my daughter as much as I could about the things that would take place throughout the pregnancy, as well as the things that would happen during labor and delivery. She then shared her fears with me – the first one being labor pains. In the middle of our conversation, she looked at me and said, "Mama, I don't want to go back to school pregnant." I could feel tears wailing up, but I fought them back and explained to her that it was June and based on my calculations, she was about six months pregnant. School was scheduled to start early August, which meant there was a strong possibility she would be going back to school pregnant. I did my best to assure her God would be taking this journey with her, but at the same time, I was careful not to build false hope. I then encouraged her to pray about those two fears specifically.

A few days later, we were sitting on my bed talking about the changes that were about to take place in our lives. I told her we would need a bigger vehicle and we needed somebody to give it to us because I didn't have the money to buy a car and I certainly couldn't afford to have a monthly car payment. She looked at me and asked, "Do you really believe that can happen?" I replied, "I know without doubt that it can happen." But even as those words rolled off my tongue, I began to question if it could. But instead of giving into the fear, I said, "God, here's your stuff! For whatever reason, You permitted this situation to be and if You had wanted it any other way, it would have been!"

A few weeks passed and we were finally making our first visit to the doctor's office. We prayed before leaving home and although she still had a few months before giving birth, included in our prayer was the fact that she didn't want to experience too much pain and the fact that she didn't want to go back to school pregnant.

Her blood pressure being dangerously high put the baby in distress and she was immediately admitted to the hospital. An emergency C-section was performed the next morning. Do you see how God answered her prayers? The emergency C-section meant her pain was minimal AND she would not be going back to school pregnant! Can you say MOUNTAIN MOVING FAITH??? I had no idea how God was going to doing it, but I knew He could if He wanted to. A few weeks later Maya was having her first feeding at home when I received a phone call and the voice on the other end said, "I have something for you and I need you to come get it." That same day I had a vehicle parked in my driveway that I paid absolutely nothing for. It was given to me – NO STRINGS ATTACHED. In the weeks following, we had a baby bed, three car seats, a year's worth of diapers and several large bags of new and used clothing delivered to us. These things happened the way they did because I didn't spend my time worrying about **how**; instead, I focused my attention on **WHO**!! The words, "DO NOT FEAR" are mentioned 365 times in the Bible. There are 365 days in the year! What are you worried about again?

Give God His Stuff

We're almost ready to start this life changing journey. Have you bought that journal I mentioned earlier? If not, step away from the book and DO IT NOW!!! With your journal in hand, go to your quiet place – that place you go to when you need to escape reality for a while. Jot down everything you need God to fix quick, fast, and in a hurry! Don't leave anything out – dig deep into the crevices and grab that thing that has slowly become a nuisance in your life. Snatch up the things that consume your daily thoughts and all the things keeping you awake at night.

Perhaps you stepped out of God's will, went to the car lot and drove home in a vehicle you couldn't quite afford, but you just couldn't live without. Maybe you closed the deal on a home in a neighborhood without God's permission, or maybe you took it upon yourself to choose your mate. Include those things too!!!

Why? Because you have no idea what do with any of it! Yes, you created these situations, but it's still not your stuff. Everything you have in your possession at this very moment is because of God's permissive or submissive will. Are there consequences for getting out of His will? Absolutely! But, it's still not your stuff!

Now that you've gathered it all up and written it all down, close your eyes, block out all distractions, and meditate on how those things are slowly separating you from God. Be completely honest with yourself and think about how your relationship with God has changed since you've been stressing over these situations. Remember self-honesty is one of the key elements to trusting God, so don't rush through this part of the journey. Take your time, be completely honest, and allow yourself to feel whatever you're feeling.

The list you've made is your daily prayer list, but before you start praying over it, take a nice long look at it and repeat these words,

God, here's your stuff!

Do with it what you will!

If only it were that easy, right? I'm not telling you this journey will be easy; I'm telling you, it'll be worth it. But here's the deal, you can repeat these words every day for the rest of your life, but they will mean nothing if you're not willing to put in the work to release the doubt and fear you've allowed to enslave you. This journey will require total dependence on God and it will require giving up some things and people you may not be ready to let go!

Day 1

The Girl in the Mirror

Preparing the Heart

Scripture to Commit to Memory

"Simpletons are clothed with foolishness,
   but the prudent are crowned with knowledge."
                                                Proverbs 14:18

Passage for Study and Meditation

"For if you listen to the word and don't obey, it is like glancing at your face in a mirror. You see yourself, walk away, and forget what you look like. But if you look carefully into the perfect law that sets you free, and if you do what it says and don't forget what you heard, then God will bless you for doing it."
                                                James 1:23-25

Guided Prayer

Father God, as I begin this journey of self-awareness and deliverance, I simply want to say, Thank You! Thank You for the opportunity to get better acquainted with You and with myself. Thank You for the desire to bury this spirit of anxiousness that constantly enslaves my heart, mind, and soul. Thank you for giving me the courage to take an honest look at the girl in the mirror. Thank you for the strength to stop running from the person at the core of my being and for the vigor to become more like You every day. I ask now that You help me to become sensitive to the changes that need to be made from the inside out and that You give me the determination and diligence to make those changes. I offer this prayer of thanksgiving and make these requests known in the strong and powerful name of Jesus. Amen!

My Heart's Response

The first day of this journey was one of the hardest for me because I was forced to take a nice, long look in the mirror and, in doing so, I was compelled to admit I wasn't in love with the girl staring back at me. There was a time when my relationship with God could not be shaken by any circumstance. I could hear His voice as if He were literally sitting next to me. There was a time when He spoke to me in my dreams and I would get up in the middle of the night to write down the messages because I didn't want to risk forgetting. But somewhere amidst all of the heartache, challenges, broken promises, disappointments and feelings of anxiety, I lost myself and my faith in God had slowly dissipated.

It was at that moment that I felt an essential need to get back to the girl I once was. I could no longer exist in a body that didn't exemplify Christ. I'm a firm believer that the people we surround ourselves with are either contributing to or hindering us from becoming the individuals we're destined to be. There is absolutely no gray area! So, I grabbed a notepad, pulled up a chair in front of the mirror and made a quick, fast and in-a-hurry list. In other words, I began to acknowledge all of the things and people contributing to my lack of faith in God. After making my list, I realized I had to rid myself of some things, but in order to do that, I had to free myself of the *root* connecting me to those things. Doing so was by far one of the hardest things I've ever had to do, but I knew it was necessary for me to successfully complete this journey. So……..I let him go! He had become a God in my life and was the root of why my relationship with God was practically non-existent.

Today's passage encourages us to examine ourselves and not only examine ourselves, but also to make the necessary changes under the guidance and direction of God. It wasn't enough for me to look in the mirror and observe that action needed to be taken. I couldn't just walk away and do nothing about it. Effective hearing – or in this case seeing – requires an appropriate response to what has been observed. Seeing required making the necessary adjustments according to the truth that I had been given. The same holds true for you! Get up! Walk to the mirror! Take a nice long look at the person staring back at you. What or who is fueling the fire to your lack of faith? The source of my hindrance happened to be an individual. That may not hold true for you, but today is the day you find out and today is the day you let it go.

Your Heart's Response

In your own words, summarize the passage. Allow it to speak to every fiber of your being. Allow it to minister to the very core of you.

What is the root of your lack of faith? What are you holding on to that's hindering your relationship with God? Is it bitterness, anger, unforgiveness, unanswered questions?

_____
_____
_____
_____
_____
_____
_____
_____
_____
_____
_____
_____
_____
_____
_____
_____
_____
_____
_____
_____
_____
_____
_____
_____
_____
_____
_____

Acknowledge that these things do exist and that they are weakening your faith and your ability to trust God's timing in your life. What action will you take to rid yourself of these things?

_____
_____
_____
_____
_____
_____
_____
_____
_____
_____
_____
_____
_____
_____
_____
_____
_____
_____
_____
_____
_____
_____
_____
_____
_____
_____

In your study, did you become aware of sinful activities you need to walk away from? Do you have the courage to walk away? If not, what's holding you back?

_____
_____
_____
_____
_____
_____
_____
_____
_____
_____
_____
_____
_____
_____
_____
_____
_____
_____
_____

How did your heart respond? Now that you know what's hindering you, outline a plan of attack. What steps do you plan to take to get your life back?

_____
_____
_____
_____
_____
_____
_____
_____
_____
_____
_____
_____
_____
_____
_____
_____
_____
_____

Day 2

As You Sow, You Shall Reap

Preparing the Heart

Scripture to Commit to Memory

"But your iniquities have separated you from God; your sins have hidden His face from you so that He will not hear."

Isaiah 59:2

Passage for Study and Meditation

"Do not be deceived: God cannot be mocked. A man reaps what he sows. Whoever sows to please their flesh, from the flesh will reap destruction; whoever sows to please the Spirit, from the Spirit will reap eternal life."

Galatians 6:7-8

Guided Prayer

Father God, as I humbly approach Your throne of grace, I ask that You wash away the guilt of my unjust behaviors and cleanse me of all unrighteousness. Thank You for yet another opportunity to be in Your presence, for I am eternally grateful for another day to give You some much deserved praise. Lord, thank You for being such an awesome God. Thank You for the Holy Spirit, who acts on my behalf when I don't know what to pray for. Thank You that when You allow pain and problems to touch my life, You always have my best interest at heart. Thank You for choosing me to be a vessel for Christ in a world where salvation is so desperately needed. I ask that You help me to walk in obedience before You and that You continue to order my steps as I strive to walk in Your will. In Jesus' name, Amen.

My Heart's Response

No one will ever know the heart-wrenching pain I felt when I heard the news that my daughter was being sexually abused by her father. Even more heart-wrenching was the day I learned I might have unknowingly contributed to the abuse. A few weeks after receiving the news and after things had settled down, I went to my daughter and asked her why she didn't come to me. *"Why didn't you tell me what was happening to you?"* She innocently replied, "Mama, I did it for you. I just wanted you to be happy." My heart dropped!

Where did my child get the idea that my happiness was more important than her safety? And just as importantly, why did she think I was happy? She didn't know I cried myself to sleep almost every night because I was being physically and emotionally abused by the same man who was sexually abusing her. She didn't know there were several nights when I was literally on my knees begging for my life. She didn't know he told me he would kill me if I ever left him and I believed him!

After hearing her truth, my wedding day and the months leading up to it slowly and vividly flashed before my eyes and reality hit me like a ton of bricks! My anxiousness and unwillingness to wait on God had put my child in danger! My refusal to trust God's timing changed her life forever! My disobedience contributed to her abuse!

A lot of you reading this will undoubtedly say that it wasn't my fault that I was physically and emotionally abused and that I didn't contribute to my daughter's abuse. You would be wrong in that assertion! I had a hand in it all because I got in a hurry. I was a single parent tired of being alone, tired of trying to make ends meet....tired in general. So instead of waiting on God, I took matters into my own hands and found myself married to my high school sweetheart who professed to be a minister, but was actually an abusive pedophile. Had I not I gotten in a hurry...had I not gotten tired of waiting on God...had I not taken matters into my own hands, my daughter and I wouldn't have experienced such traumatic events.

And when it was all said it done, I lost everything. But this time was worse than before. My children and I had to move in with my mom, I didn't have dependable transportation, and I had Child Protective Services *breathing* down my neck. But all of this could have been avoided if I had just waited....if I had just trusted in God's timing! I left God no other choice but to reprove me. But even in my disobedience, I turned my circumstances over to God. In other words, I gave God His stuff, knowing He could handle it far better than I ever could. Justice was served for my daughter and when the time was right, God blessed us to move into a place of our own and provided me with reliable transportation.

Many of us foolishly believe God's love for us is so great that He'll ignore our indiscretions and lapses in judgment. God chastises those He loves. This means, there are consequences for stepping out of His will. As affirmed in today's passages, sin hinders our blessings because we're no longer trusting and relying on God. Sin also separates us from God, thwarts our ability to hear His voice and contrary to what some believe, forces Him to reprimand us. With that said, some of the struggles we encounter are directly related to our unwillingness to trust God. But, here's the good news....... You can still experience God's love & promises even when you're sure that you don't deserve them! It doesn't matter what you've done! He hasn't written you off! He hasn't counted you out! FORGIVENESS IS JUST A CONFESSION AWAY – restoration awaits you!

Your Heart's Response

What role have you played in your current circumstances? Did you get tired of waiting on God and took matters into your own hands?

_____

What stuff do you need to give to God as a result of that?

What steps can you take today to remedy the situation?

After careful examination, is your faith being challenged or is God reprimanding you for stepping out of His will? Is a request for forgiveness in order? If so, now is great time to make your request known.

What's hindering you from confession and restoration?

Day 3

Struggle is Necessary

Preparing the Heart

Scripture to Commit to Memory

"In the world you will have tribulation; but be of good cheer, I have overcome the world."
John 16:33

Passage for Study and Meditation

"For His Holy Spirit speaks to us deep in our hearts and tells us that we are God's children. And since we are His children, we will share his treasures – for everything God gives to His Son, Christ, is ours too. But if we are to share His glory, we must also share His suffering." **Ephesians 8:16-17**

Guided Prayer

Father God, thank You for another chance to get better acquainted with You. Thank You for looking beyond my *I want it now* attitude and for the insight to recognize that my trials are essential to my spiritual growth. Thank You for the assurance that victory is on the other side of my tribulations. Thank You for Your consistent and deliberate love as I learn to trust Your timing and rest on Your promises. I ask that you anoint my mind with wisdom, knowledge, and understanding as I strive to become the person You've destined me to be. In Jesus' name. Amen!

My Heart's Response

I have the pleasure of ministering to some amazingly awesome girls. During one of our bi-monthly RAP sessions, we played a game where we had the girls pull a question from our *question vault*. Upon pulling the question, the girl had the option to answer or pass. One of the questions pulled was, "If you could ask God anything, what would it be?" Needless to say, she chose not to pass up the opportunity to ask God a question. What child would? The question was, "Why is life so hard?" She sat in the circle anxiously waiting for me to address her question. There were twelve eyes staring at me with great anticipation and I felt like everyone was screaming, ANSWER THE QUESTION, LADY!!

Because I was completely caught off guard, I found myself struggling to answer her question. I thought I'd buy myself a little time by asking why *she* thought life was hard. She then began to tell me how her mom had been in a car accident and couldn't work. She expressed that there were days when there was no food for her siblings and her. Her response made the question more difficult to answer because I had asked the same question several times for some of the same reasons.

Although not her exact words, I felt like she was asking me why bad things happen to good people. In an effort to comfort her, I began to share some of my personal experiences about how God brought me through some rather trying situations. But even while sharing with her, my mind wandered to a few weeks prior when I was going through a struggle of my own. I was lying in bed talking to God about my situation. I recall telling Him my life wasn't supposed to be like this. God then asked me a question, "Why is your life not supposed to be like this?" That painstaking question was indeed a wake-up call for me. It was a reminder that God never promised me a life free of trials.

Turn your attention to these words in today's passage, "And since we are His children, we will share His treasures -- for everything God gives to His Son, Christ, is ours too." Focus on the latter part, "everything God gives to His Son, Christ, is ours too" – not some things – EVERYTHING! Everything means the whole thing – not bits and pieces of it – not the parts we like, but instead all of it.

Sadly, some of us think being saved comes with a *get out of hell free card*. Quite the contrary, my dear! Salvation is free, but that doesn't mean our lives will be free of trials. As a matter of fact, Paul says, "But if we are to share in His glory, we must also share in His suffering." We don't get to choose the parts we want to share in. That means you need to get rid of the image in your head of how your life is supposed to be; trust your struggle, and remember that trials are a necessary part of the *everything* and know that victory is on the other side.

Your Heart's Response

Do you think your life is hard? Why is God allowing *bad* things to happen to you?

_____
_____
_____
_____
_____
_____
_____
_____
_____
_____
_____
_____
_____
_____
_____
_____
_____
_____
_____
_____
_____
_____
_____
_____
_____

Do you have an image in your head of what your life should look like? How is that image affecting your relationship with God?

What spiritual growth have you experienced as a result of past struggles?

How can your current struggle be a blessing to others?

What will you do today to embrace your current struggle?

Day 4

It's Going to Happen Suddenly

Preparing the Heart

Scripture to Commit to Memory

"All these blessings will come on you and accompany you if you obey the LORD your God."
Deuteronomy 28:2

Passage for Study and Meditation

"Count it all joy, my brothers, when you meet trials of various kinds, for you know that the testing of your faith produces steadfastness. And let steadfastness have its full effect, that you may be perfect and complete, lacking in nothing."
James 1:2-4

Guided Prayer

Father God, thank You for the wisdom to recognize that every challenge, every struggle, and every tear I shed has a purpose. Thank you for counting me worthy to stand on the frontlines of a battle that has already been won. Thank you for using my current circumstances to show Yourself strong in my life so that your glory will be revealed to those who don't believe. Thank you for the reassurance that You are there in the midst of every storm. I ask that You give me the courage to stop swimming against the tide and ride the wave out! Help me to relinquish the spirits of fear and defeat that I constantly allow to hold me captive. Give me the strength to fight with diligence and in such a way that those on the outside looking in will know it was You and only You who brought me through. In Jesus' name, Amen.

My Heart's Response

September 30th, 2008 was one of the most memorable days of my life. After constantly moving from one rental property to another, I was finally signing the closing documents to homeownership. My children and I were over the moon excited about this amazingly awesome blessing. We were moving to a much nicer neighborhood with better schools and the house was more spacious than any other we had lived in. We were in house heaven! We spent the weekend unpacking, organizing, and basking in the awesomeness of God. Much to my surprise, I was quickly knocked off my homeownership high! The following Monday I found myself sitting across from my supervisor listening to her tell me I would be unemployed effective October 31st due to company layoffs. All kinds of questions started racing through my head. *What am I going to do? How am I going to pay the mortgage? How do I tell the children? God, what are you doing?* After asking countless questions, I began the rationalization process. *I'll get unemployment benefits. The mortgage is not due for another month. I'll have a job by then. It's all going to work out. God wouldn't give me this home just to take it back. Girl, get it together! God's got you!*

Well, things didn't quite work out the way I played it out in my head. God blessed me and I started a new job December 1st only to be laid off four months later. Only this time, I didn't get any kind of notice. I reported for work only to be told they could no longer employ me because of company cutbacks. My faith wasn't as strong this time. I had no idea what God's plan was and I was in no mood to try and figure it out. So, I went home and had a good old fashioned pity party. *What kind of God would shower me with blessings just to take them back? I was striving daily to walk in His will. I was doing all the right things! How dare He treat me this way!*

As months passed, with only unemployment benefits as income, the mortgage fell into default, was on the edge of foreclosure, and my faith was growing weaker every day. I was diligently seeking employment while working an unpaid internship to satisfy graduation requirements for my undergraduate degree. On the days when I wasn't doing that, I was sending e-mails and making phone calls to anyone who would listen to my story in an effort to save my house. I reached out to foreclosure prevention organizations, bankruptcy attorneys, and the mortgage company, but to no avail. And then it happened. I received a letter in the mail with an auction date for the sale of my property. My heart dropped! My faith was weak, but I refused to give up! I started crying out to God like I never had before. Stretched out on my bedroom floor with tears flowing from my eyes, I screamed to the top of my voice, "GOD YOU HAVE

GOT TO MOVE! You promised me that my children and I would not have to move again and I promised my children the same thing based on the promise you made to me! God show yourself strong in our lives right now!" I don't how long I was on the floor. But when I got up, I had an answer on how to save my house. God laid out a plan so clear there was no way it wouldn't work. I grabbed my laptop and began a google search for the CEO of the mortgage company. I found an e-mail address and under the direction of God, I started typing. I told my story just as God directed me, which included the promise I made to my children. I prayed over the e-mail and clicked send. Can you say mustard seed – mountain moving faith? I received a call from the CEO within a few hours of hitting the send button. She listened to my story and promised she would do everything in her power to make sure I didn't lose my home. A week later, I received a call for a job interview. A couple of weeks later, I was employed making more money than I asked God for and six years later, I'm still in my home! It all happened so suddenly, I didn't have time to question whether or not God would honor His promise!

Today's passage encourages us to count it all joy when trials come upon us because the testing our faith brings forth persistence. Each time we overcome a trial, our faith grows stronger. Some things we experience are for no other reason than to grow our faith so that God gets the glory. No matter what you go through, you have to know that God has your back. And when it's all over, the naysayers – the ones who laughed at your pain – will have no other choice but to acknowledge that it was God who brought you out! God's desire is for us to use what He has given us to further His Kingdom and proclaim His glory. It's what we were created to do. So even when you want to give up, you can't! Because if you do, God gets no glory.

Your Heart's Response

What challenges are you facing today to grow your faith? How are you handling the challenge? Are you on the verge of giving up?

_____
_____
_____
_____
_____
_____
_____
_____
_____
_____
_____
_____
_____
_____
_____
_____
_____
_____
_____
_____
_____
_____
_____

What spiritual activities are you engaging in to pass the testing of your faith?

How will God be glorified when you come out on the other side?

Are there times when you feel God has forsaken you? How are you handling those times?

Can you recall a time when God delivered you suddenly? How is that situation a reminder of what God can do in your current situation?

Day 5

Just Say the Word

Preparing the Heart

Scripture to Commit to Memory

"Though you have not seen him, you love him, and even though you do not see him now, you believe in him and are filled with an inexpressible and glorious joy."
I Peter 1:8

Passage for Study and Meditation

"That day when evening came, he said to his disciples, 'Let us go over to the other side.' Leaving the crowd behind, they took him along, just as he was, in the boat. There were also other boats with Him. A furious squall came up, and the waves broke over the boat so that it was nearly swamped. Jesus was in the stern, sleeping on a cushion. The disciples woke Him and said to Him, 'Teacher, don't you care if we drown?' He got up, rebuked the wind and said to the waves, 'Quiet! Be still!' Then the wind died down and it was completely calm. He said to his disciples, 'Why are you so afraid? Do you still have no faith?'"
Mark 4:35-40

Guided Prayer

Father God, thank You for yet another day to increase my knowledge of faith. Thank You for the assurance that Your Word holds true today just as it did yesterday. Help me to exercise my faith by simply taking You at Your word and obeying the commandments You have clearly laid out for me. Give me the strength needed to walk steadfastly in faith, knowing it is essential to this Christian journey. Help me to trust Your direction even when I don't know where You're leading me. Help me to recognize that it all begins and ends with You. In Jesus' name, Amen.

My Heart's Response

Besides the Bible, my absolute favorite book is the dictionary. When my children were younger, we often had *Mr. Webster time* at the dinner table. Each of us would choose a word from the dictionary, read the definition and then use the word in a sentence. They weren't crazy about it, but I was having the time of my life because I love learning new words and dissecting them to get to the root of what the word really means. As much as I love analyzing and interpreting words, I've never fully examined the word, faith…until now.

Without question, we've all been asked the question, what is faith. If you happened to be sitting in Bible class or Sunday school when asked, you and all of those in attendance most likely boldly and proudly replied, "the substance of things hoped for, the evidence of things not seen." We've all been guilty of it and I'm not implying that doing so is incorrect. However, in order to get a full understanding of faith, we need to scratch beneath the surface.

Earlier this year I was in the middle of a huge transition in my life and much to the surprise of others, I was at peace with it. I wish you could have seen the looks I received when I told people I wasn't worried… the looks I received when I said, "God's got me." They couldn't understand the peace I had as I was waiting to start my new journey under the direction of God. They couldn't fathom how I was rejoicing in the midst of what appeared to be a storm. They didn't understand because they didn't know my story! They didn't know how long I had been praying about the situation. They didn't know how many times God has brought me through…how many times my life had been turned upside down and how each time I literally thought I was going to lose my mind.

But as the day of that major transition began to slowly approach, I started to gradually lose sight of those things as well. I was slowly but surely going into panic mode. My salary was about to be cut in half. The mortgage, car payment and a stack of other bills would still be coming in like clockwork and I had two children who depended solely on me for support. I was still excited about finally being able to devote some serious time to my God inspired calling, but I had no idea how I was going to make the salary cut work for me. So in an effort to hold on to my dissipating faith, I began to do a little research on the word and came across the story of the centurion who strongly believed Jesus could heal one of His dying servants. The centurion said to Jesus, "Just say the word, and my servant will be healed." Jesus then turned to the crowd following Him and said, "I say to you, not even in Israel have I found such great faith" (Luke 7

NVIV). In this passage, Jesus seems to imply that great faith is simply taking Him at His Word. I thought, *it can't be as easy as "just say the word." If it were, everyone would be exercising great faith.* My disbelief led me to what I like to call the *New York Best Seller* for faith, the Book of Hebrews. Chapter eleven of this book references several individuals who had simply taken God at His word. Each individual's name was preceded by the words, "By faith." Each person mentioned defied personal feelings, reason, and logic. Each named individual simply took God at His Word.

I still wasn't convinced that having faith was as simple as *just saying the word*, so I kept digging and came across today's passage where Jesus had just finished a full day of preaching and teaching by the shores of Galilee. He instructed the disciples to go to the other side of the sea. In the beginning, they took Jesus at His word, got into a boat with Him, and headed for the other side. But when a storm arose, they grew fearful and lost confidence that they would actually reach the shore. When Jesus asked them, "How is it that you have no faith?" In other words, "Why are you not taking me at My Word?" If you read on to chapter five, you'll find that they made it to the other side. This, of course, means that Jesus' Word proved to be true.

Not to my surprise, Jesus' Word also proved to be true in my circumstance. As difficult as it was, I stopped doubting and took

God at His Word. My salary was indeed cut in half for three months and not one bill went unpaid and not one bill was paid late. I am now convinced that faith IS just saying the Word! It's saying, "God, I know you've got my back and I trust that Your Word is true." Faith may never know where it is being led, but it knows who's leading. Faith is holding God's hand in the dark and trusting that you'll come out safely on the other side!

Your Heart's Response

Have you taken the time to dissect the word "faith" to determine how important it is to your Christian faith? Now is a good time to do so.

In your daily walk, how often do you find it difficult to simply take God at His Word? What will you do today to remedy the situation?

What will it take for you to relinquish that spirit of doubt and fear so that you'll safely come out on the other side?

How can today's passages help you take God at His Word?

Create a daily affirmation as a reminder that faith is just saying the word and taking God at His word. Write about how that affirmation will help you in your daily walk with Christ.

_____
_____
_____
_____
_____
_____
_____
_____
_____
_____
_____
_____
_____
_____
_____
_____
_____
_____
_____
_____

Day 6

Trust the Process

Preparing the Heart

Scripture to Commit to Memory

"Trust in the Lord with all your heart and lean not to your own understanding; in all your ways submit to Him and He will make your paths straight."

Proverbs 3:5-6

Passage for Study and Meditation

"So I went down to the potter's house, and I saw him working at the wheel. But the pot he was shaping from the clay was marred in his hands, so the potter formed it into another pot, shaping it as seemed best to him. Then the word of the Lord came to me. He said, 'Can I not do with you, Israel, as this potter does?' declares the Lord. 'Like clay in the hand of the potter, so are you in my hand, Israel. If at any time I announce that a nation or kingdom is to be uprooted, torn down and destroyed, and if that nation I warned repents of its evil, then I will relent and not inflict on it the disaster I had planned.

Jeremiah 18:3-8

Guided Prayer

Father God, here I am once again before Your throne and today I simply want to say, Thank You! Thank you for just being you. Thank you for reminding me that You are the potter and I am the clay. Thank You for challenging my faith. Thank You for loving me enough to uproot and tear me down as often as needed. Thank You for working behind the scenes, for protecting me, and for fighting battles on my behalf. Thank you for the strength to lean not on my own understanding and for the power to trust Your process. Thank You for the process that it takes for me to become the person I was born to be. In Jesus' name. Amen.

My Heart's Response

I'm a single parent and I have been for most of my adult life. Even when I was married, I was still *kind* of single...but that's a story for another day. I have four beautiful girls and a handsome son. They've all contributed to a few of my gray hairs and I've spent a number of sleepless nights worrying about each of them at one point or another. But it was different with my son. I think I was a little harder on him because I was determined to make sure he was a better man than the man who contributed to his existence. In other words, I was determined to make a man out of him!

I didn't want him to become like the boys he often kept company with. I didn't want the streets to get him! I didn't want to lose him to drugs. And then it happened! I lost him! I lost him to it all and I didn't know how to get him back. So I did what I do every time my back is up against the wall. I cried out to God and prayed the hardest prayer I've ever had to pray. My prayer was no longer God make him the man he's destined to be; it was now, God, do whatever you need to do to save my son. I took my hands completely out of the situation and I went into prayer for him like I never had before. *God, do whatever it takes to save my son.* At the time, I had no idea how powerful that prayer was – I just knew I needed him back. Within months, my son, at the age of seventeen, was facing a thirty-year prison sentence and I found myself questioning God daily. *What are you doing? This is not what I asked for! I didn't want him incarcerated. I just wanted him obedient and at home before curfew. What are you doing?* It was then that God reminded me of my prayer. You see, I didn't specify how I wanted him saved. I said the word and God did as I requested.

Needless to say, I was distraught over the possibility of my son living thirty years of his life behind bars. But as much as it pained me, my heart knew confinement was exactly what it would take to save him. So against the better judgment of my flesh and some family members, I decided against hiring an attorney. Sure enough, he was sentenced to thirty years in prison and I thought I was going to lose my mind. My heart ached for him. My soul cried for him. But most importantly, my spirit prayed for Him!

Take a look at today's passage. When Jeremiah arrived at the potter's house, the potter was diligently working at his wheel. If a pot turned out badly, he would simply start over – using the same clay to make another pot. That was his process to turning the clay into a beautiful masterpiece. In the same way the potter works on his clay, God works on us [his children]. The testing of our faith is God molding us into the persons we're destined to be. The passage goes on to imply that at any moment God can decide to shake things up a bit. The consequences resulting from our disobedience is God shaking things up a bit. This passage is a reminder that God, reigning in sole sovereignty, has the right to deal with His children in any manner He chooses. In other words, we don't get to tell Him how to fix the situation. We don't get to tell Him how long we should be in the storm. He can change our circumstances whenever and however He chooses.

Regardless the situation – a testing of faith or a shaking up of things – we must recognize that God is the potter and we are the clay. This means He has the power to fix that which has been damaged or shaken up and He can do that however He sees fit. By the grace of God, my son only served three years of a thirty-year sentence. As a result of my obedience, my son is now being shaped and molded into the man God would have him to be. If I had not trusted the process, I could have very well been burying him instead of visiting him behind bars.

Your Heart's Response

How often have you questioned the Potter's process? How difficult was it for you not to fix the situation?

_____

Are you seeing clearly enough to recognize that God is molding and shaping you into the person you're destined to be?

Write about a time when not trusting the process ended with dire consequences. Knowing what you know now, what would you do differently?

_____
_____
_____
_____
_____
_____
_____
_____
_____
_____
_____
_____
_____
_____
_____
_____
_____
_____
_____
_____
_____
_____
_____
_____
_____
_____
_____
_____
_____
_____

Write about a time when your prayers weren't answered exactly as you had hoped. What were the results?

Day 7

The Answer to Why

Preparing the Heart

Scripture to Commit to Memory

"That you may be children of your Father in heaven. He causes the sun to rise on the evil and the good, and sends rain on the righteous and unrighteous."

Matthew 5:45

Passage for Study and Meditation

"To everything there is a season, and a time to every purpose under the heaven: A time to be born, and a time to die; a time to plant, and a time to pluck up that which is planted; A time to kill, and a time to heal; a time to break down, and a time to build up; A time to weep, and a time to laugh; a time to mourn, and a time to dance; A time to cast away stones, and a time to gather stones together; a time to embrace, and a time to refrain from embracing; A time to get, and a time to lose; a time to keep, and a time to cast away; A time to rend, and a time to sew; a time to keep silence, and a time to speak; A time to love, and a time to hate; a time of war, and a time of peace."

Ecclesiastes 3:1-8

Guided Prayer

Father God, thank You for the final day of this seven-day journey. Thank you for the lessons learned and the opportunity to dissect and digest your Word daily. Thank you for the journal entries that will serve as reminders of why struggle is essential to my growth in You. Help me to apply these teachings to my daily life and help me to walk through every challenge with my head held high. Place someone in my path that I can be a blessing to simply by sharing my testimony of faith. When I'm faced with some of the most difficult challenges, help me to remember that to everything there is a season and a reason. In Jesus' name, Amen.

My Heart's Response

"Does everything really happen for a reason or do people just say that to make themselves feel better about the things (good or bad) that happen in their lives? Sometimes I say that when things happen to me and then later down the line I try to figure out what happened as a result of it; I can never really think of anything. So once again, does everything really happen for a reason? Everything I'm going through right now, why is it happening? I can't figure it out. But then again, maybe I shouldn't be trying to figure it out. But I really would like to know if that saying is true. I believe it's just a quote for comfort. You say that to your friends when you want to make them feel better about something that happened to them and you tell yourself that when you want to do some self-comforting. So is that saying really true or is it just something to help us with the everyday happenings of life?"

I was taken aback when I received this question via e-mail from a teen I was ministering to because I've often found myself asking the same question on numerous occasions. However, when I'm confronted with a rather trying situation, I've learned to do a little soul searching. I start off by asking myself if the situation is a result of some unwise decision I've made. I begin there because I believe some things happen simply because of cause and effect. It's kind of like the old saying, "What goes around, comes around." In other words, you reap what you sow. Not to my surprise, many of the things I've gone through are because of things I did or didn't do according to God's Word.

I'm not saying that's the case with everyone, but it may be helpful to search your own heart before looking for answers elsewhere. If you can truthfully say that you did nothing to cause your present circumstance, try a different approach. Instead of asking every why question imaginable, ask what. *What is the lesson to be learned? Lord, what are you trying to teach me?* Sometimes the Lord is trying to teach you endurance; sometimes He wants to teach you how to totally rely on Him. Or perhaps, He wants you to know that He can comfort you and heal you as no one else can. Whatever the case may be, know that everything does indeed happen for a reason—not your reason, but God's.

The enemy wants us to believe that God is unjust and that He forsakes us when we need Him most, but it is he who is behind the scenes working overtime to bring harm to us. Today's passages affirm that there is a time and a season for everything and that God rains on the just as well as the unjust. To expect things to remain the same in a world where change is constant is absurd. To expect a picture perfect life in a world of imperfection is beyond ludicrous. To expect God not to challenge our faith or chastise those He loves will only lead to a life of disappointment. To expect an answer to each of life's questions is foolishness. Sometimes the only answer to why is the lesson learned and we must learn to be okay with that.

Your Hearts' Response

Do you believe everything happens for a reason? Elaborate on your answer.

_____
_____
_____
_____
_____
_____
_____
_____
_____
_____
_____
_____
_____
_____
_____
_____
_____
_____
_____
_____
_____
_____
_____

In your honest opinion, what is the reason behind your current circumstance?

Do you really need the answer to why? Explain your answer.

How has this seven-day journey impacted your life?

What is your go-to passage when your faith is being challenged? Why?

Not in Working Order

I Bounce Back Every Time the Devil Knocks Me Down. Oh, what a powerful phrase! But how many times have you been knocked down and felt like you would never get back up? Some time ago, the Lord gave me the awesome task of writing about being broken. I would love to say I was eager to dive into this assignment, but the truth is, I put it off for several months; as a matter of fact, I didn't just put it off – I totally disregarded it and had pretty much made up my mind not to do it. I would rather have been disobedient and suffered the consequences than have to deal with areas of my life that I had closed the door to and had no desire to revisit, but the Lord had different plans.

As I embarked upon my assignment, I immediately ran to the dictionary to define the word "broken." Webster actually has quite a few synonyms for the word; some of which include: violated, ruined, interrupted, and not in working order. When I first saw "not in working order," I thought hmmm—I like that, "NOT IN WORKING ORDER." Then I began to question whether that was the proper way to refer to someone who's experienced traumatic events in their life. Just as I was about to give up on using it as my basis for defining being broken, the Lord brought to my attention a time when the faucet in my kitchen sink was broken. When the problem began it was just a really slow, but annoying drip…….. drip…….. drip then it turned into drip, drip, drip and after that the water began to slooowly run and I had to work really hard to turn it on or off, until finally the faucet just completely stopped working.

Some of you may be questioning what a broken kitchen faucet has do with an individual being broken. Allow me to paint a picture. If you've ever experienced anything traumatic in your life, you know what it's like to be broken and confused; and you know it's not always easy to stand firm on your faith in Christ. In many cases, your flesh begins to ask every why question imaginable and the last thing you want to hear is "God has a purpose and a plan" or in my case "All things work together for the good…" You want answers and you want them *yesterday*. And when you don't get answers or if you're not satisfied with the answers given, you begin to slowly pull away from God, instead of drawing closer to Him. Here's the completed picture. That really slow drip is you easing away from God, the somewhat faster drip is you walking a little faster to get away from Him, and little by little you begin to slowly run further and further away until eventually you've completely stopped running to Him and your family and friends have to work really hard to get you to acknowledge His existence.

Let's face it – if you're not running to God when tragedy strikes, you are definitely NOT IN WORKING ORDER. I can say that because I've been there. I was saved at the age of fifteen and had a faith in Christ that could not be shaken — or so I thought. But approximately seventeen years later, I found myself engaging in activities I never thought possible because I allowed my circumstances to break me and separate me from the God. Suddenly, I was drinking alcoholic beverages day in and day out. I was taking pills to go to sleep at night and more pills to stay awake during the day. Most of the time, I wasn't aware of my existence in this world. I was no longer complete—I was not in working order.

Romans 3:23 reads "All have sinned and fall short of the glory of God." I am no exception to the "all" that Paul refers to here. Although this verse in written in past tense, it is a well-known fact that we [Christians] continue to sin. There have been many times in my life when I have allowed life's circumstances to separate me from God. However, it was during those circumstances that I realized my life does not work without Him. He completes me. Without Him, my life has no meaning. There have been times when I've been burdened down by life to the point where I had no desire to pray. During many of those instances, I would crawl into my bed, curl up in fetal position, pull the covers over my head and with tears rolling down my face, I would pray, "Lord I need you to rock me to sleep tonight, but please don't wake me in the morning." As selfish as that request was, God, in all of His awesomeness, wrapped His arms around me, rocked me in His bosom and in a still small voice whispered, "You can do this." During these burdensome times, I never recall falling asleep, but I remember slowly opening my eyes to daylight peeping through the draperies and thinking to myself, I can make it through another day.

I am so very thankful that God is not a pass or fail God. He knows I will fall, I will make bad choices and yes, I may even fail. But as wonderful as He is, even when I fail...even when I make bad choices and even when I fall, He picks me up, nurses my wounds, rocks me in the cradle of His arms and in a still small voice whispers, "You can do this my child."

When you are not trusting God, when you are not standing firm on His promises, you are not in working order! Whatever your struggle, whatever the circumstance preventing you from trusting God with your life, know that God is still on the throne and He knows what you have need of before you even ask. When you learn to give God what belongs to Him, He will perform miracles on your behalf.

It All Works Together

As evident in the preceding readings, the challenging of faith is a necessary part of the Christian journey and it has its purpose in more ways than one. By now, you have undoubtedly come to realize that my faith has been challenged on numerous occasions.

There were times when my faith was strong enough to overcome the challenge, and there were times when my faith fell short. But through it all, I learned that my reaction to the circumstance was totally dependent upon me and it is only by the grace of God that I'm still around to tell my story.

My prayer is that this devotional has been a blessing to you in your efforts to trust God's timing in your life. I encourage you to boldly take God at His word knowing that every challenge you face is working together for your good!

Thank you taking this journey and for allowing me to be your tour guide. This is only the beginning of your transformation. When you feel like you're at the end of your rope, remember these teachings and my testimonies – and remind yourself that God is the potter and you are the clay!

****

Faith Reminders for Life's Challenges

God keep me from trying to do YOUR job, help me to do YOUR will, assist me in doing MY part so that you get all the glory!

Insufficient faith has proven to lead to insufficient funds!

The enemy wants you to believe it's the end, but it's not over until God says it over!

You know you serve an awesome God when He can create a day to meet each of our specific needs!

Feel the fear and do it anyway!

God is not a man, so He does not lie. He is not human, so he does not change his mind. He has never spoken and failed to act!

The devil in hell can't keep you away from your destiny if you know who you are in Christ!

About the Author

Shirley is a self-proclaimed *microwave girl* who is using her newly transformed *microwave* mindset to make over the lives of individuals everywhere! In a world of instant gratification, instant food, instant messaging, instant EVERYTHING, Shirley speaks from her life experiences to empower individuals with the tools needed to change a *microwave – I want it now* mindset into one of patience and endurance.

She has been anointed with a unique ability to tackle issues ranging from the acceptable to the seemingly taboo. She will challenge you to come to a firm understanding of what you believe, why you believe it and how those beliefs line up with the TRUTH of God's Word. She has a broad range of experience that includes life skills training, youth leadership, workshop facilitator, motivational speaker, youth mentor and faith coach. Her daily mantra and message to the masses is TRUST THE PROCESS! It is her sincere desire to see followers of Christ walking ON PURPOSE into their God-given destinies!

She is the creator of themicrowavegirl.com and is a powerful voice that the Lord has raised up to touch and dramatically change the lives of all of those she encounters. Her message is as passionate as her testimony is transparent. Having overcome so many of the struggles and assaults that plague society today, she teaches out of her own personal experience and wisdom. The negative microwave mindset that she once so fearlessly embraced, is now, by the power of God, being converted to one of irrefutable trust in God's timing.

For speaking engagements and other events:

Email: Shirley Hubbard - info@shirleyhubbard.com

For additional copies: www.amazon.com

If you found value in what you've read, please take a few minutes to post a short review on Amazon.com!

Thank you for your support!

GOD, HERE'S YOUR STUFF

www.ingramcontent.com/pod-product-compliance
Lightning Source LLC
Chambersburg PA
CBHW060844050426
42453CB00008B/822